Your

Strange

Fortune

PAST

PRESENT

FUTURE

NOW

PAST

> "If you look too often to the past, you'll never see where you're going."
> —Fortune Cookie, circa pre-collapse

Automatism; or What to Visit in My Town

There was a woman
kept hands
lined up in jars
along her walls

Hands of children,
                men,
                        crones—
from soft to ridged
with wrinkles, from having spent
so much time holding the hands
of others

These hands, she showed
to visitors—prized as needle-
point portraits or tea cups
imported from some place
exotic—and they would gasp
and ooh ahh, such
perfections

Once or twice a visit, someone
recognized the fingers
of a former lover, the heart-
line of a childhood best
friend, the bird-fine wrist
        of a piano teacher,
                once desired,
the way she pressed keys, hovered
hands over—

The woman would ask
if the visitors wished
to borrow, or buy,
        but no, no
                heads shook
        hands pushed deep
        into pockets, don't
        be tempted.

Still, the collection grew
        hands floating,
                fingers stretching,

as if to reach
     out and grasp
         another's.

Like Acheron but Not

My sister told me once that she
made a river
when she was young
she told me how she dug
her fingers through the ground
till water welled like blood
from her scalp after running the comb
in her hair too hard.

She said the river
smelled of damp, rot,
dust, the inside of treasure
chests in the rain-felled
house. And the river
was the color of rust water
finally run clear but she knew
that it held rust once.

She said it sounded
like bells underwater,
the kind fish might hear if they were
called home for supper
and that it tasted of the forest
after the burning, the pavement,
the parking lot formed.

She asked if I wondered
what the river felt like.
I wondered how
the river dreamed,
what it remembered,
who it longed for.

She asked again
but I shook my head
afraid that she
might tell me the river
just felt cold.

Mirrors are Practically Useless to Me

we crack our knuckles back to the bone, bend our wrists forward
and backward and place our palms down on tables, we twist
them clockwise to read the time, we know all of the names of all
the bones in our hands, they are precious and important and
each one plays a role, we can slip our hands free from handcuffs
and spread decks of cards out like fans, we know how to feel the
number of them in a deck and count them up

taste the words on the tip of your tongue, swirl them in your
mouth, spit them out or swallow them back, incantations taste
like cake, like scones dripping with butter and honey fresh from
the oven, and the honey gets on your fingers, lick it off and the
sweet sticky taste will remind you of telling stories as you lay
the cards out, the king and the queen go into the forest and
bandits appear and the queen is safe in the castle, but can we
make her reappear

stretch out your body on the floor, arch your back, plant your
soles on the ground firmly, try to raise yourself, try to raise
yourself is what Hansel and Gretel's mother told them when she
pushed them out the door, and the stones clinked in his pockets
like they were keeping musical time, he laid them out and sure
birds ate the crumbs, but why did nothing eat those stones,
shining like light under the moon, and were there no ghosts who
would take the pebbles and swallow them one by one in hopes
of getting that light back and count off to your

favorite number, show the card to the audience, tell them to
memorize it, have someone, a stranger, take the card and rip it
into pieces or drown it in water or devour it covered in
chocolate syrup, dunked in red wine, and watch them savor it,
then shuffle, shuffle, cut, false cut, reshuffle, have someone else
take the deck from you, have them flip the top card and it is
always the card returned, so expected as to be unexpected, no
one thinks the tricks will fail anymore

what do you do when you never slip, when every trick works,
and you dream at night of piercing bodies with swords, of
escaping knots underwater, of palming coins until the end of
your life, what do you do when even in your dreams the girl is
never left in two, the knots always tug loose, the coins never fall

with a clatter to the floor, what do you do when there is no trick
left

place your hands on the floor, stretch out the muscles of your
body, speak lies to fill your patter, taste the words, they taste
like grass, like cinnamon dusted snow

we all wait with breath held, with eyes unblinking, and we
disappear slowly, tying the ropes around our wrists, dipping
backwards into the water, pretending we know the answer to the
riddle, the answer is smoke and

Boy Meets Monster

There are so many stories
about those who go out
into the world and save it.

Of King Arthur and Beowulf
and Odysseus and all
those seventh sons of seventh sons.

What, though, of those boys
who see the monsters and think
nothing of them? Who shake

hands with devils? The ones
who look at pictures, under horrific
headlines, and think that no

one should be punished for
a single mistake? Returned
to lore, to fable, we try

to remember the boy
who fought monsters
because they were so easy

to spot.

Rat-Infested Ghost Ship Off the Coast of Britain

Bones in this ship
clitter-clatter and teeth so sharp
they make marks, map our hunger
across the white, off-white, bones
the color of cream just gone
sour sweet, oily on the tongue

Water is rocking us, waves are holding
us, keep us close, this wind makes lullaby
through the eaves, our mothers sang
tales to us of blades and mirrors and lovers
who turned to marble, to pebbles, to
beasts, and we slept like ice babies

like those ice babies left in the cradles
for mothers to find in morning time, melting
to puddles, that is loss made for children's ears,
ice babies, changeling babies, and we dreamed

of children to love us, to hold us close, name us
and feed us biscuit bits, crumbs off fingertips,
take them soft and nibble nibble

at my house, at my ship, is it a little

we scatter and sway, our legs sea-worthy,
our nails dig in wood, we wait and
watch, the water goes on, the water
is the sky is the water and we wait

we wait

They said we ate our children, our
siblings, but we eat only the dead,
we can taste their dreaming, we are the
dead, we are the living, the lived in, sweet
and sour

coats our tongues.

I Believed Not in God but in Gods as a Child

And apocalypse? Apocalypse was just
the fact of life. Those bodies lined up
on the front yard never looked more beautiful than
in that dreamless sleep. Oh, they felt so
cold. We washed their hands until they
glistened, kissed
the lips hard of the young men who couldn't feel it, caressed the brows of the young
women who couldn't know it, and blessed them all with names they couldn't refute.
We cannot possibly
bury them all they
told us and so we lit pyres. The flames
danced differently with this new form of fuel that
we fed them, oh, higher and fuller of
grace. I wanted to hold hands with someone
but no one
was there who could clasp
fingers. The smoke stung my eyes to salty tears and the ash colored my hair; I looked
aged a hundred years and almost ready to turn to dust.
Their belongings we sorted
into piles. The clothing was ragged, every
pocket had a hole. I found one tiny
notebook, worn
to softness and most was smudged away
except the letter 'I'
and I wondered if it was the
word. What was useless was burned, paper starts the quickest. As a child I warmed
myself by the fires we had stole out of them.

The Body Turned

He told me that it was what teeth
were made for: the tearing, the pull.
We were made to devour.

I think of you most when I'm falling
asleep on boats in the middle
of the ocean and I remember
that some people even eat
squid, the ink blackens
their teeth, and some eat
lions, and...
oh my.

He told me that my hands were made
for searching, he could read it in the lines
stretched taut across my palms, little
trip wires of the life laid out before
me. He said I should stop, give
in, and taste something hot
and sharp on my tongue.

I think of flesh and muscle and bones
and veins and the pulsing beat
of a heart. It reminds me of the taste
of ash, of the memory of dust,
of the color of the eyes of the man
I was meant to marry in the ghost story
dream I used to have.

He told me that meat is sweetest
caught fresh, and from something
wild. He said you could taste
the freedom in the flesh.

I think of a deer running,
the trees made blur, the sun
dipping low enough to kiss, the deer
runs and runs. I remember the sound
of the mother deer calling out, rage
and loss, as the coyotes circled the twins.
She scared them away with her yell, those
wild dogs sent away.

He told me he could taste the freedom,
sweet upon his tongue, I stare out
the window, watching the sun bleed

into the forest.

Once for Yes and Twice for No

The Fox Sisters were known for their ability to speak with the dead. They listened to the rap, rap, raps of the spirits knocking on walls, on tables, on the inside of cabinets. The raps were letters spelling out secrets. They said a man had been murdered. Buried beneath their house. Such secrets. Secrets

are better left unsaid. Sometimes, Maggie and Kate Fox would try to close doors, cover their ears, not listen. The public called for more, for more, voices like pounding. The taste of alcohol was sweet compared to the pounding. Maggie dreamed of the sky

bleeding into her skin whenever she went out at night. The stars in her veins shimmered and fell. She didn't ever wish upon them. What could she have wished for? Kate began to manifest the spirits onto stages across America. They shimmered and shook. The spirits never

asked for much. Rapping, rapping. After years, the sisters finally admitted to fraud. The rapping merely the cracking of their toes done in unison. "We only wanted to play a joke on Mama," they said. Voices shaking

Years later, children playing in the ruins of the old Fox house found white sticking out of the ground. So chalky-colored, so smooth. The bones of a man, murdered some said.

Turtles and Hares

There once was a woman
who found skulls buried
beneath sand, she was looking
for seashells and found molars,
incisors, sockets where hazel
eyes once were. She unearthed
them gently—she feared a skull
might disintegrate as easily as the once
lived in shell of a horseshoe crab.

A boy chose to swallow a key.
He felt it unlocking the bones
of his trachea. It tasted of
metal but also of divinity—
that sugary candy foam his mother
once stirred above the stove for
what seemed like hours.

There was a village where one
of every family lived. They gathered
the bones of their loves and buried
them three feet deep. The key
swallowed by one fell through
the bones of a ribcage and turned
eventually to rust and then to nothing
ever again to be found.

The Escape Artist Ponders Mortality

My hands are tied
           you say
my body is captured
           and there is nothing
                      I can do to escape

You are always saying lies
           built upon facts
there are so many chains
           you wear and that wear you

Underwater, even, you are a half-truth
           as shiny as the pins you hold in your mouth
the metal tastes sweet on your tongue
           and you always wait a little longer
                      every time

Longer to free yourself, longer
           to burst back into the air
to meet the gasping crowd
           and their applause always
                      sounds so far away

Your ears pop underwater, holding
           your breath, but you can
hear your own heart beat so clear
           pump pump pump
                      pump pump

And when you finally surface
           and the air fills your hungry lungs
it takes you a moment longer
           every time, to remember
                      that your heart sounds like

someone pounding at your door.

Collective Color Constancy

In this light the dress
is blue and black

                    I'm sorry
When you are falling backwards
you will remember that white and gold were the color of the stars, hung from the
ceiling, at your third grade birthday party and you will think to yourself that you
should have said thank you more throughout your life, thank you to your mother who
cut stars from leftover wrapping paper for hours, and thank you to your best friend
who braided your hair that morning and thank you to the clerk at the dress shop years
later who said that the dress looked nice on you

                    I'm sorry
The dress is blue
and black

                    I'm sorry
You saw your own reflection in the window and jumped, startled, because you never
expect to see yourself looking back at you, and the phone rang at the same time, and
picking it up you said hello in a breathless way and no one was on the line, except that
you could hear something, someone singing in the background, and you thought it was
a pocket dial, until you recognized the song as the one your grandmother used to sing
to you when you were little and trying to go to sleep but you'd fight it, you'd fight the
sleep until you just couldn't anymore, and your grandmother sang of fields of gold and
white clouds

                    I'm sorry
The dress: blue
black

                    I'm sorry
When you know no one will catch you
you try to save yourself, grab at something, but your hands connect only with air, and
you think of the color of your best friend's hair, flax, no gold, gold sounds prettier,
and her dress was white and she was running in front of you and you reached out to
grab her arm, and stars, and your grandmother singing, and fields of gold, and clouds
of white, and stars

                    I'm sorry
Black and
blue

          and

                    the dress
                         looks beautiful on you

PRESENT

"Outlook good."

—Magic 8-Ball, circa today

Stricken

We buried our dead   but first we wrapped them tightly in white
the shrouds kept the souls locked up, tight, and comfortable   The plague-dead
we called them, as if so much different from the other dead

bodies are bodies
the earth will return them to dirt just the same   Shrouds keeping them longer
        maybe
        or not   The dead rise and white cloth hangs from the body

                        Our ghosts are tricks   sheet swaddled children
trundling from house   to   house asking for treats   something good to eat
        mothers hold the hands of their children tight, the grip loosening only at
doorways, when it's safe, when they are asking for gifts, baskets outstretched, mothers
breathe out and watch their breath hover in front of them, the cold bites as the sun dips
low, children dressed as the dead turn back to smile

Caskets were too needed to bury, carried the bodies over and over, the dead in their
shrouds would be protected enough.

                        he grave is cold, the cloth clings.

So many we buried, one by one by one by one by one by one by one, no time for rites, for
prayer, and the dead in their shrouds, shook and shuddered beneath the earth.

A mother finds the drawings later, of ghosts hovering, like sheets filled with air, and she
traces   the   image   with   her   fingers   The
indentations make the drawing seem fresh   She can feel them The sun has a
smiling face   Her daughter's hands did this

                        The shroud memories are carried, like the dead
themselves were carried, into the present   These ghosts drawn in sheets, white shrouds
rippling around shapes that once held life   Children come to think of ghosts as white
and bright

        Children who survived the plague, years later, remembered the images of
skeletons   dancing with the rotting dead   sheets covering bodies but
not the death itself
                        We buried our dead   We bury our dead
            wrapping them tight   hoping to keep them warm

The Double Dark Theory of Our Universe

I too believe that our lives are
not as interwoven as we are led to
believe, that you and I were
only coincidences in the other's
timeline. Still, something

as simple as the entanglement
of our fingers reminds me that
once I felt entirely safe within
your world. Do you often, also, think

about black holes? How they taste
and swallow all the stars in their
path? Sometimes, when I see
you in a crowd, and I pretend
not to, I remember the way you

looked the last night I saw you
and you said in another life
we would be happy. And I said
in another life we would be

free from one another's ghosts.

Googolplex

We type: can you kill yourself
with apple seeds? Why can't we
sleep in beds not out own? What was
that film about a jewel heist, a woman
in topless car, black-and-
white? Around the table, remnants

of potato tacos, salsa cruda, decorate
plates, and we ask
questions. Try to sort out what we
know from what we think
we know from what we want
to know.

Pushing close together, we stare
at phone screens, watch videos
of people testing the limits
of their bodies. One of us

says: I used to think I knew
so much, but, Jesus,
there's so much more. Clear plates,
slice chunks of cake to eat

while wondering aloud. Powdered
sugar dapples the table, our fingertips
and lips. We say: what else
can we look up? What else
can we discover? Our breath

is catching in our throats,
we are killing ourselves
with curiosity
being sated. That saying,
what is it, curiosity killed—

But, where did it come from?
We can look that up next.

My Year as a Medium

I once went home to find the dead crowding into my bed. They tossed and turned all night, stole the covers, talked in their sleep. They said the names of lost lovers over and over until I almost believed that they were people I too had lost. Sometimes I dreamt the same dreams as the dead. They dreamt as one and I fell into them as easily as one might fall back into the bed of an ex-lover who you never see but still remember the breath of against your skin.

They dreamt in tastes. Pulling candy down from off the top shelves. They were so sweet. Tiny chocolate bears with tummies of milk. Placed them on our tongues and let them melt. The sugar was electric. It caused us to shiver. Of the taste of river water gulped, of the taste of tea leaves bitter and rich and filled with the future, of the taste of sweat off another's skin.

They dreamt in sounds. It comes to us like flashes of ecstatic light, the blood of saints, the way it wraps and breaks us up. Of the sound of rain echoing down the sides of the house, of the sound of whispers into ears and the breath was hot against our skin, of the sound of palms being read in the version of our lives where every line stretched on forever and wrapped around our hands over and over again.

They dreamt in lightning and ice and the electric pulse of skin meeting skin.

They dreamt of hands.

Of mouths and lips.

They dreamt of silence and the way dirt tasted so bitter and salty.

The way that ashes sound.

I wished I could sleep at night without their arms embracing me; they seemed so cold and, yet, still burnt me to fever. I wished I could sleep without the weight of them surrounding me.

They dreamt of silence but screamed at night. I was no comfort to them, so I just dreamt along.

I left them once for days I spent pacing with open eyes; they seemed to forgive me for this. Please forgive me for this.

Cups are Always Falling, Breaks are Always Close

slipping from my hand as I slipped
from my footing and the world caught up
to my body, sometimes, falling

I remember that life is a series of
falls: you fall in love, you fall out,
you fall into line.

I've fallen in life more times
than I care to think about: broken
bones, snapped tendons, ligaments torn,

memories shaken from the places
I kept them. On the ice, pieces
of my cup scatter the ground—

Picking up the fragments,

I think of when you once told
me that you had a habit of leaving
things you cared about

in hotel rooms and bus stops,
places you'd never return to.
You said, "Sometimes loss just feels so good."

And it had made me think
that one day I might want to forget
so many falls. That they could form scars.

Later, I will pull a shard of porcelain
from my fingertip and there will be
a split second before

the blood wells out, when
I can imagine that I might
never bleed.

Sleepwalking

Don't wake him, that's the first thing you think
when you find your sleeping lover walking
through the house at night.

Remember your cousin, when
you were eight or nine, who told
you about a boy who was woken
while sleepwalking, and the shock
killed him. Dead, right there, boom, your
cousin said, smacking her hands together.

Your lover washes his hands at the sink,
eyes closed, and you wonder
what he is dreaming about, cooking?

Remember the time you dreamed
about standing in a kitchen at night and your
great grandmother, years in the grave,
sat at the table, asking you to make
potato pancakes with sour cream and chives.

But, you only had a fridge filled with asparagus
and lemons. In dreams you should, at least,
be able to please the dead. And sitting
down beside your great grandmother
you began to weep, and she cradled you in her arms.
The tears sustenance enough.

Your lover walks to the window, still
sleeping, and presses his forehead to the glass.
You wonder if the cold would wake him. Then,
you notice he is crying. Tears from out of his
closed eyes.

What dreams do we dream, you wonder, when
we think we are unwatched? You want to hold
him, lead him back to bed, but don't wake him,
you think. Let him
sleep.

My Life Had Stood a Full-Court Press—

At some point, you realize
your hands are bleeding

bleeding from infinitesimal
cuts all over your palms

your palms which once so tenderly
held a basketball, even spun it on one

one fingertip, the kind of trick
you had learned young, never forgot

forgot like so many other things:
color of her hair, smell of catalpa leaves

leaves floating into view, the slow-mo
replay of the ball arcing into net, smooth

smooth as glass, the cuts on your hands
are bleeding and you can't remember

remember where you are, some accident,
some screech of wheels, break of glass, back

back of the board, clanging off, spin
around hoop and points, points

points as the buzzer sounds, the siren
gets closer, louder, and you have won

one lucky guy, they'll call you later
and you can do nothing but agree.

Hum

Whales can no longer speak
to one another beneath the waves
or rather it is understanding
each other that they have lost.

The simplest messages
have become poems in dead
tongues, hieroglyphic symbols
for species that no longer
exist and so are translated
as myth or mistake.

And now when the whales give
themselves names
the sound each makes
can call out to no one.

Still they send echoing
hellos down long abandoned
tunnels where the only answers
they can hope to receive
will come from ghosts.

Tricks to Keep Away the Dark

We've been eating oranges
until our mouths go numb

sticky juice coats our
hands, our lips

sweet and sour and

we've been told that citrus
keeps the spiders away,

the moths from cupboards
and the ghosts from

under the bed,
sliding out incorporeal

shadow-long fingers
reaching up to tangle

in our hair, but no
longer, we spit orange

seeds onto wooden floors,
run our hands down

each other's bodies

proofing the skin against
the touch of the dead

we feel safe when we
taste one another

and we feel safest
when our mouths are numb

Missing Girls, Continued

My best friend swallows needles
while we sit beside one another
in the dark, watching static

flicker on the television. She says
do you remember

that boy in grade school who let
go of the merry-go-round? Someone
found his tooth embedded in concrete
days later. I say isn't it miraculous

we all survived childhood? She turns
to me and I see through her emptied
out eyes, all the way to the back

of her skull. Where does she store
her memories now, I wonder. And she
asks me if I think about when her parents

called me late at night and asked if I knew
where she was. I want to say, there is nothing
else that I think about more. But that's not

true. I often have the same dream, many
nights in a row, and in it we are staring
up at the night sky, counting all the shooting
stars that ice their way across the blue

but we forget to make wishes, too busy
thinking of how the stars must have
names, we just don't know how
to say them.

Filed Under Hazy Creatures

They lived above me, those two
and spent the days leaning over
the balcony, watching the parking
lot. I'd walk the dogs

below them. The dogs' nails clicking
against the pavement. They'd lean
over more, gaze on the dogs

and once I heard them talking.
What is that do you think? asked
one. The other, the one with
the band t-shirts always on, replied,
I think it's like a wolverine.

The first craned his neck out more,
staring at the dogs. No, dude,
because that would make it, like,
half cat.

I will remember this years later
and catch myself willing to
believe that sight can make
such errors—this
bestiary of the false.

Pre-Game Pep Talk

Listen:
think of yourself as the arc of ball
to hoop, think of yourself as the points
not the miss. Think of yourself as the Reggie
Miller eight points in nine seconds, think of
yourself as a Wilt Chamberlain 100 point
game.

Try not to think of yourself as Rasheed
Wallace's back at the end of his Celtics
run, how he winced so sharp.
Don't imagine yourself as anyone opposite
Robert Horry in the last minutes of a close game.

Think of yourself as movement
on the court: as a dribble, a jump shot,
a slam dunk. Try to avoid being the hard foul,
Shaquille O' Neal on the free-throw line, Chris
Webber calling a time-out.

Try to remember that there is no over
until the clock runs out. Everything comes
down to ball through air, swish through net,
points changing on the board.

Space Like Hands

you know they found a chupacabra
not far from where I live

and the body, because it was only
a body lost of life not living still,

made the newspapers, at least
the local ones with the letters

to the editor always about school
assemblies and church parking

lots. It seemed so tiny
in the photo like a mouse

baby dropped from its nest
but the caption claimed it bigger.

I wondered what the skin
of a chupacabra might feel like—

leathery or soft as bat wings
and the inside of dog ears.

Later the laboratory examining
the remains declared it was only

a malnourished raccoon and they
destroyed

the body.

You Told Me To Check the Facts and Read the Numbers

You burn 26 calories every minute
that you spend kissing someone. It doesn't
matter if their mouth tastes like hot chocolate,
those calories will still be lost.

And women have more taste buds
than men do, so that chocolate
is extra bitter, extra sweet.

And on earth there are roughly 265
people born every minute while
115 die. So, really each loss we feel is a
gain to someone somewhere.

Half of the people who die
at the blast of a bomb
are the ones who were trying
to make a bomb and 40% of murders
occur during arguments and both of
these statistics are sad in
different ways.

1 in 5 marriages end before the
fifth anniversary and more than 99%
of species that have ever lived,
over all of time, are extinct.

The longest kiss on record
lasted almost 31 hours. That's 213, 900
people lost. And still we keep kissing, passing
our hearts back and forth like playing
cards, Go Fish.

Aura Symptom

Sometimes I imagine my body as a part
of someone else's house
a room where the ghosts are stored
in rows, organized alphabetically or,
maybe, by color or shape

When a lover once traced my bones,
his hands warm and the pressure precise,
he said that he could feel fissures
under my skin, as if my body was breaking
slowly from within

And I often talk to strangers,
in the library or on the bus or
in aisles of the grocery store that I need nothing
from, and ask them to tell me if they can see
whether or not I'm still here

Z is for—

When my sister came back
from the dead, we watched her
first tentative steps as if she were
a baby on the verge of toddlerdom.

Please, she said. That was it, though,
we waited for her to continue.

She was so cold, we wrapped her
in blankets, tucked hot water bottles
under her feet, made steaming cocoa
that I decorated with the heads
of marshmallow Peeps.

Please, she said. Her tongue was thick,
the word came out funny, foreign.

We watched the undead on screens,
movies where we used to flinch and scream,
videogames where we used to blast their
rotting bodies with shotguns.

Please, she said. Her eyes saying
something else, but we'd never been good guessers.

We brought her food, she should eat, she
needed to eat, but she shook her head, pushed
away our arms, tried to yell, but nothing came out
but a moaning, the sound in films that would
be accompanied by dragging footsteps.

On the screen, she jabbed her fingers at
the undead being shot. She said, please.

On a Watermelon Truck, With a Chupacabra

North from Texas, the smell
of rinds like fresh-mown grass,
sweet and contained

Chupacabra dreams of cool
air, against furless skin, and dew-
soaked leaves

In Texas, a woman puts out steel
traps to catch chupacabras, fills
the cage with spicy Cheetos and wet
cat food, a mingle of salt and rotting

Chupacabra curls smaller, size of one
prize-winning melon, tries again to
welcome sleep, one husk of fruit
in one small paw, savoring pink chunks of flesh
for days, fruit born of heat that tastes
of cold

In the south, chupacabras are a menace,
blood thirsty, vermin; guns are loaded,
traps are set, the livestock must be protected

Chupacabra watches the land flashing
past, desert gives to lawns gives to cornfields
gives to trees, Chupacabra licks juice
from sticky paws

One man says a dead chupacabra is worth ten
living, he taps his foot and points at a bounty
sign he designed himself, a chupacabra drawn
with fangs bared, claws out, wild

As the truck slows, Chupacabra leaps
and lands, dashes to the darkness of forest
cover, still holding three black seeds, memory
that out of sand can grow water

Sometimes We Searched the Ground for Feathers

We plan our vacations
around things we don't believe in.
In Scotland, once, we traipsed
the skirts of Loch Ness
and bought up postcards
with blurry photos of what
could never have been there.

In Ireland we wish
to visit the island of Saint
Patrick's Purgatory. It is where
he banished
the Cornu to—the final home
of a giant, terrifying bird.

We love the promise of myths,
but every year there are others,
people who reach the island
on pilgrimage. They fast
and they endure the cold
in order to cleanse
themselves of sin.

We imagine ourselves among them
with our guide books and cameras.
We wonder if we might
ever just give in to something—cast
our sins with our doubts
that we counted as our own
rosary beads.

Would the Cornu accept us,
if that is what his purpose is,
to take the memories
we want to free ourselves from
and eat them up?
The only birdseed we think to scatter.

The Other Side of This is Still Here
"The optimist proclaims we live in the best of all possible worlds.
The pessimist fears this is true." —James Branch Cabell

You asked me if I considered myself
an optimist or a pessimist.
I told you I'm an optimistic pessimist,
always hoping for something better.

The truth, though, is not exactly that.
When I was seven, swimming, I nearly drowned,
pressed down by undertow, but lucky,

a precocious reader, I remembered
that the key to surviving the pull
of waves is to give up, don't fight,
let your body go limp. And so

I lived. This is a story I would
tell you, if we were closer, I'd
say the sky through the water
was the color of an emerald

though when I think about it
that can't possibly be true. It's
the way I remember it, like
how I'll remember you, years

from now, as someone I once
reached towards though I should
have known you were too far
away.

FUTURE

> Catch a star, catch a star
> Yesterday you were a dove
> Throw it far, throw it far
> now you know who is your love
> —Children's Fortune Telling Game, circa After

Metal Lark

Let the birds scatter
themselves, wings clicking
like beads strung loose
upon a thread, and realize

that there are still some colors
we cannot make from jars. If
feathers can scratch, sculpted
fine from metals, then how

many will it take to build
the bird? Wind up the key,
turn a thousand times or more,
and let loose the clockwork

nightingale. Place paper
nests amongst the highest
tree branches, eventually
they will be filled

with marbles like eggs.

La Città in cui io abbia abitato

Why are abandoned cities so creepy? I asked without expecting an answer. Is there anything more rhetorical than our definitions of the dark? How to explain

the color of your eyes at sunset. Do they always blink so? Do they always fall in and out of your face like yo-yos of light? Do you always mean to stare right through me and point to the mural behind me? Do you mean to describe with such clarity the colors I'm standing in front of? I'm here I'm here

here is where the heart is. You can hear it beating. Here hear. Do you notice the voices between the beats. They are calling out the name of your lover. The one you left at the bottom of an ocean, the one you left at the bottom of it all, the one you left with her heart spinning out of orbit. She wants you to know

I thought I heard you yesterday, walking behind me for a block or so. When I turned there was no one there except of course there is always someone something there

tell me about ghosts again. They are coming through the walls at night. They are

listing their favorite things: coffee ground fortunes and hard candy fish colored like rainbows, like the inside of the sky in your dreams, like did you ever imagine as a child what a cloud looked like on the inside, like the inside of the fox skull you found one summer, half hidden under leaves and dirt and

here are cities laid out, destroyed, watch the tide come in, watch the tide come in, watch the tide come in, watch the tide come in

how many places do you know abandoned? Count them. Tell them you'll remember them. Tell them you know the names of every place you will ever long to see again and they are always on that list. Tell them

that question is still rhetorical and I am hoping to hear you respond.

Generations

We watch tides roll backwards
water the color of blood
oranges and thick enough
to float our bodies on the surface

Millions of miles
from where our parents came
they guide us to these beaches
tell us don't go in

but they have told us stories
of the water back home, their
home, water so clear that fishes
can wink up at the sky

and we imagine cold, cool,
imagine dipping our toes,
wading up to our knees,
sinking into the deep

Don't, our parents scold,
pulling us back from red
water, bleeding shores,
grip our arms so tight

the marks stay for days—
reminder that we are home
and it is far from any place
that our parents actually love

Museo de Spazio

In our museums there are rooms
and rooms filled

with the things we could not bear
to leave behind us:

pieces of highways, signs
for businesses long since

consumed by roots of trees,
one single spike from Lady

Liberty's crown. In one
thousand years, children

will press noses against
glass and stare at the shoes

worn by Judy Garland
as Dorothy Gale and the

children will marvel at
the sparkle, at the things

we took so far. They will
read the signs on glowing

plaques: there is no
place like home.

Please

Mother says remember
she says the Earth was once an hourglass
and we kept turning and turning
it until its shape twisted,
formed something strange

Mother says be witness,
as she plaits our hair, she says
spread these stories out into the wilds
of planets far beyond the stars we
know, the ones we name easily

Mother says dream deep,
taste the edges of the rivers
that no longer run, their bodies
thick with sludge, mouths
coughing up refuse

Mother says honor the dead
but don't be lost in them,
those birds whose skeletons
spread across shores, those
landscapes left wanting

Mother says push
forward, promise to keep
moving, seeking, dreaming,
imagine that there is something
left that we have to give

Other Ways of Mapping Constellations

Whose hands bleed flames, those
fingertips hot, skin against skin,
and the mark they leave is not of ashes,
and the weight of the world is almost
a candle. When we spread secrets back
and forth between us, they taste
of the night sky, of sweat, of sweet.
Have I ever told you about the time
the stars had teeth, they devoured galaxies
in their sleep, accidentally almost, and black
holes were left gaping and we had to fill them
with memories, and retellings of fairy tales,
and knock-knock jokes that no one ever got
the punch lines of. And speaking to each other
we imagine the shape of mouths more even
than the words, the shape of lips, the movement
of tongues. Who is left wanting, aching, rising,
waiting, and each movement feels like the moment
before release. You speak of flames, of fire, of heat,
the pulse and push of a breeze as it carries us closer
to one another. We leave our bodies at the gate
of the night and try to remember what we named
ourselves, so that we might recover our own
shells eventually upon waking.

This Song is the Same Song, You are the Different One

The end of the world comes in waves.
                Cities that crumble. Children who turn into birds. The Eifel Tower
                rusts overnight.
No, wait.
                All the dark says is
                Be still, be still.
The end of the world comes as a fire.
                Everything is reduced to ash. Even the ocean is pool of silty
                silty water.
No, wait.

                Mothers want to hold their children close,
                Imagining their lives, if the world did not end:
                Kindnesses they could have done, the people they might have
                Loved, cherished, grown apart from, because even in loss
                Music can be found.
The end of the world comes as darkness.
                We wake up one morning and the sky is the color of
                a pupil at the center of an eye. All the light pulled in.
No, wait.

                Mothers sing quiet lullabies that they
                remember from their own youths.
                There is no remembered voice as lovely
                as your mother singing you to sleep.
The end of the world comes as silence.
                Everyone speaks but the words reach the ears of no one.
                A tree falls and everyone is there and it still makes no sound.
No, wait.
                The world undoes itself, the children vanish, the motherswatch the
                news in horror, the maps X-ed out of existence, the
                young are swept into war zones where no one ever sings away the
                dark.
The end of the world comes and no one understands.

Sidelong Catastrophe

I'm not sure who the sky is
when it's not the sky

but I think I know this river
was once a beautiful woman

viewed from above all bodies
of water look like someone

you once loved and the color
of the trees only matters

when there are trees at all
and sometimes I imagine

that we can solve everything
design cities that fit into

the Earth instead of making
the Earth fit into them

but mostly we sit at drawing
boards and paint scenes

of decay because that is what
we know and sometimes I think

I can see the sky but
it might just be a person

and I'll miss the sun most
when the clouds weep the ghosts

of rivers for days on end

Ballad of Silver Blades

I'm sure your ghosts will come
out of the corners of rooms
and the backs of closets, hidden
behind coats that haven't been worn
since they were in style that year
everyone wore yellow the shade
of marigolds.

Your ghosts will answer to every name
that you think to call them. Remember
how it felt the first time you realized you
never knew the middle name of your
grandfather? Ghosts will still answer, even
if all you call them is *love* or *you there*.
Ghosts carry no grudges, they can't
keep up with them.

You will always wonder what became of your ghosts,
the ones you heard singing in the hallways
of emptied out buildings, the ones who
had such beautiful voices but only when
they thought no one was listening, the ones
who hummed instead when they saw you
could see them.

One day you will ask for your ghosts
and your voice may shake and your
breath may come too fast, too shallow,
and you will wonder what time it is where
they are and whether they might
catch their trains, walk the distance,
reach you soon enough. Know, though,
that I'm sure your ghost will come,
they will always come, to hold you
as tightly as they can.

The Rhyme We Told as Children

If I admit to you that there will always be at least twelve seconds taken from every day because I think of you then what exactly am I admitting to?

And what of buildings abandoned? Of places let to go dark?
He told me to write about something haunted. I saw you in the shadows once. Running around corners and dust shook from your clothes. He told me to imagine the corners of rooms and what might be waiting for shadows to come back to them. He told me that where there were faucets running there would also be lights flickering and my face in the mirror would never be the same one I thought I should see staring back at me.

If I say that the last time I saw you I tried to count the beats of your heart and lost track and somewhere in that losing I just lost everything?
And what of those stone stairwells and basements and stalls with locked doors but no one inside? Of sound echoing back to you but not the words you spoke aloud?

He told me to think of stars falling and how they must have felt scared at first and then delighted by the sudden cold. He told me that wishes were like ghosts and if you didn't believe in them then they couldn't come true. It hurts to think about the way I thought you were starlight slipping through the window. There are rooms in houses with no windows and the light still gets in. It hides in corners and waits for the creaking of doors, for the faucet running, for the tap tap tap.

If I tell you the truth but only in a language of the extinct will you hear it? A language spoke underwater, at the bottom of wells, inside of mirrors? And what of the corners where there is no place to sleep? Of those rooms where no one ever comes out or goes in but you can hear the rooms breathing?

He said to think of things that scared me. The ghosts I kept as children. Don't we all keep them? Those ones we expect in every dimly lit bathroom with the mirror that flickers? The ones we know in our closets and under our bed? The ones who like to tell us stories we can't hear because we don't speak in the tongues of the dead but still we hear them somehow when we sleep and dream of mazes and forests and planets made empty? Finally I remember the prompt. He said to write about something haunted. So I wrote about you.

Flora and Fauna of the Outer Rings

There are trees that bloom only once a year
    bursting into colors that the mind cannot
        comprehend. Guidebooks tell us
            not to stare too long, to look
                away as soon as our minds
                    begin to fizz. The first
                        sign is when you
                            start to think
                                in tastes,
                                    the book
                                        warns.
                                You will
                          remember your
                      mother's bread, fresh
                  from the oven, the crust crackly
              and butter melting, dripping down
          your hands, and honey, oh honey, so sweet
      and rich. Clover honey, it tastes like the inside
    of a golden bell. Pull yourself back, shut your eyes
  if this has begun, if you are already salivating then it might
be too late. You are already so close and the blooms spin.

The flowers close shut.

Fairy Tales & Other Species of Life

Under the gaze of snakes and spiders
we dip our fingers into soil
dig deep enough to feel the dirt
pulsing against our skin

Once upon a time someone said
and we all turned to listen
because stories beg to be heard
because in fairy tales the water
heals and the forests are filled
with mothers returned as trees

Once upon a time this land
was filled with life once upon
a time the roots of trees stayed
firm in soil and babies were born
squalling for mothers and they
were sung lullabies and everyone

Hush someone else said we don't
want to hear what has been we need
to hear what is coming

And we looked up to the stars
to the deafening dark and the spiders
and the snakes were just shadows
things used to be feared that now
were just missed

We dug deep and pushed seeds
from locked away vaults
into the earth so gentle we pushed
and we wondered if the past
could be reborn

And we whispered to the not
yet born grow
grow
once upon a time you would
grow

NOW

"...."
—When you asked what would happen

In Gratitude

On the bus, this morning,
a man talked about narrowly missing
death. "The deer totaled my car but
the semi obliterated it." There were
only moments between him getting
out of the car and the slamming crash.
His airbags never went off, the passage
out was easy. The bus driver said, "Man,
you're lucky
to be alive."
And I am thinking that there is this
in all of us:
a need to thank our luck.
In places, around the world,
the death toll rises and we
whisper prayers for safety,
for safety, for
a way to find our luck
and keep it in front of us,
an orange triangle set up
in the road, to say, "danger,
stay safe, pass around
even this."

Acknowledgments

This book is about apocalypse but the book, and my life, would not exist without kindness. I have been so lucky to be supported by some amazing people while working on this book.

Freddy LaForce and Vegetarian Alcoholic Press were an absolute dream to work with. It was incredible to feel so supported.

The editors and staffs of the magazines where some of these pieces originally appeared are often unpaid volunteers who put out incredible journals solely for their love of writing and reading, which is a true gift in this world. I am thankful to the editors, staff, and readers of the journals where the following pieces originally appeared:

"Automatism" in *Lockjaw*

"Like Acheron But Not" in *Booth*

"Rat-Infested Ghost Ship" in *Liminality*

"I Believed Not in God but in Gods as a Child" and "Cups are Always Falling Breaks are Always Close" in *Birds Piled Loosely*

"The Body Turned" in *Bombay Gin*

"Once for Yes and Twice for No" and "Stricken" in *Cheap Pop*

"Turtles and Hares" in *Vending Machine Press*

"Collective Color Constancy" in *spy kids review*

"The Double Dark Theory of the Universe" in *Pidgeonholes*

"My Year as a Medium   " in *Ghost City*

"Sleepwalking" in *Gulf Stream*

"My Life Had Stood a Full-Court Press—" and "Tricks to Keep Away the Dark" in *Hobart*

"Hum" in *Tenth Muse*

"Missing Girls, Continued" in *Public Pool*

"Filed Under Hazy Creatures" in *Stone Boat*

"Space Like Hands" and "Metal Lark" in *Abyss & Apex*

"You Told Me to Check the Facts and Read the Numbers" in *Verse Wisconsin*

"Aura Symptom" in *Noble/Gas Quarterly*

"Z is for—" in *Best Horror Poetry Showcase* and *Undead!*

"On a Watermelon Truck with a Chupacabra" in *Sleet*

"Generations" in *Recompose*

"Museo de Spazio" in *Wizards in Space*

"Please" and "Fairy Tales & Other Species" in *Sunvault*

"Sidelong Catastrophe" in *Reckoning*

"In Gratitude" in *Half Mystic*

Some of these poems also appeared in my chapbook, *The Science of Unvanishing Objects*, from **Finishing Line Press**

I am so thankful for professors and colleagues and friends who have made my writing and life better: Marc Seals, Ron Wallace, Debra Marquart, Ned Balbo, Lindsay Tigue, Charissa Menefee, KL Cook, Deanna Ward, Sheryl Kamps, Deanna Stumbo, Volker Hegelheimer, Tina Coffelt, Crystal Stone, Matty Layne Glasgow, Ana Hurtado, Connor White, Molly Backes, Jordan Kurella, Sarah Chase Crosby, Kirk Wilkins, Meghann Hart, Maria Haskins, Kathryn McMahon, KC Mead-Brewer, Cathy Ulrich, Rachel Mans McKenny, Claire Kruesel, Jennifer Hutchins, Maria Rago

I am grateful for my family, with all my love: Mama, Papa, Mike, Gabe, Jack, Kimberly, Henry, Westley, Rowan, and Millie Hatch

And my in case of apocalypse dream team, I am so lucky to have you all in my life: Stephanie Gunn, Brontë Wieland, Erin Schmiel, Philippe Meister, Brian Ramos, Tony Quick, Ean Weslynn, Hannah Cohen, Teo Mungaray, and Sara Doan.

www.ingramcontent.com/pod-product-compliance
Lightning Source LLC
Chambersburg PA
CBHW080602030426
42336CB00019B/3303